DEN
BUILDING
CREATING IMAGINATIVE SPACES
USING ALMOST ANYTHING

JANE HEWITT & CATHY CROSS

Crown House Publishing Limited
www.crownhouse.co.uk

Published by
Crown House Publishing
Crown Buildings, Bancyfelin, Carmarthen, Wales, SA33 5ND, UK
www.crownhouse.co.uk
and
Crown House Publishing Company LLC
6 Trowbridge Drive, Suite 5, Bethel, CT 06801-2858, USA
www.crownhousepublishing.com

First published 2016

p. 131 (igloo den) – photos by kind permission of Jeni Johnson,
Worsbrough Common Primary School, Barnsley.
pp. 67–69 (miniature town) – photos by kind permission of Andy Harris.

British Library of Cataloguing-in-Publication Data
A catalogue entry for this book is available from the British Library.

Print ISBN 978-184590952-9
Mobi ISBN 978-178583036-5
ePub ISBN 978-178583037-2
ePDF ISBN 978-178583038-9

LCCN 2015953358

Printed and bound in the UK by
Gomer Press, Llandysul, Ceredigion

CONTENTS

CARDBOARD BOX DENS   15

TABLE DENS   71

INDOOR DENS 81

OUTDOOR DENS 105

EXTREME DENS 129

GETTING STARTED

Welcome all new den builders!

Building dens is really easy when you know how. It doesn't cost lots of money – you can use items that are readily available around your house (check with grown-ups first though – they can become quite grumpy if you cut up their best duvet cover to make a roof for your den!).

You can create dens on your own or with groups of friends. Grown-ups will be desperate to get involved – it's up to you if you let them join in or not. (Sometimes they can be really helpful!)

So what is a den? It's a space that is separate, a space that you create for yourself, a space where you can use your imagination, a space where you and your friends can play and be creative. It can be fixed or transportable, huge or miniature, indoors or outdoors – basically it can be anything that YOU want it to be.

Where could you create a den? Wander around your home to begin with and make a list in your sketchbook (see Project 1 for a description of how to make one) of all the great places you could build a den. How about underneath the stairs or the kitchen table? In the corner of your bedroom or behind the sofa?

The next step is to begin collecting den-making materials (the resources section has ideas to get you started). You will find lots of ideas in this book about what to use, how to fasten everything together as well as how to stay safe.

The coloured boxes
each tell you something
different:

YOU NEED

Things you need
to build your den

TOP TIP

Ideas to help you

REMEMBER

Things that
you need to be
careful about –
safety tips

Now let's look at the materials you can use to get den making.

Plasma Ball

RESOURCES

RESOURCES

These are examples of materials you can use when building a den, but a creative den maker like yourself can learn to adapt anything!

- Blankets
- Bottle tops
- Boxes – all shapes and sizes
- Branches and twigs
- Broken household items – clocks, keyboards, etc.
- Bubble wrap
- Cable ties
- Cardboard – tubes, boxes, sheets
- Chalk
- Clips (e.g. paper clips, bulldog clips)
- Clothes line
- Craft knife (but only with a grown-up present)
- Cushions
- Duvets
- Fabric
- Felt pens
- Hula hoops
- Leaves
- Lights (e.g. fairy, rope, tea)
- Mirrors
- Paper
- Pegs
- Pens, pencils and paint
- Pipe cleaners
- Plastic strip door curtains
- Play-dough
- Sponges
- Stickers
- String
- Tapes (e.g. masking, gaffer, sticky, decorated)
- Tinfoil
- Toys
- Umbrellas
- Velcro
- Wooden crates
- Wool

FASTENINGS

Lots of the resources listed on page 7 can be used to fasten parts of your den together. In many places masking tape or gaffer tape will be fine, but in other places – such as outside or next to a brick wall – you will need to get creative with cable ties, hooks, string or a clothes line.

The photographs on these pages will give you some other ideas!

HULA HOOPS

Hula hoops make great fastenings for dens and can be incorporated into your design. They are easy to use and can be decorated in lots of different ways. For example, try weaving using your hula hoop as a frame or tie strips of material to your hoop to make a curtain.

If you cover your hula hoops with see-through plastic (or sticky-backed plastic), once you have decorated them they will look beautiful when light (natural or from a torch) shines through them.

Now you have a space in mind and some materials – what are you waiting for? Go and build a den!

YOU NEED

Felt pens/pencils

Two pieces of cardboard

Sheets of paper

String, ribbon or wool

OR scrapbook/ notebook

PROJECT 1
SKETCHBOOK

Building dens is a great way to stretch your imagination but you will find it helps to keep a sketchbook or scrapbook of your ideas. (You can see examples from the pages of our sketchbooks throughout this book.)

You can easily make your own scrapbook using two pieces of cardboard, string and scraps of paper. Just punch some holes in the cardboard (these will be the covers of your book) and the paper using a hole punch – making sure the holes line up – and then sew the book together using the string. Make sure you knot the ends tightly so it doesn't come undone. Easy! Alternatively, you can buy a notebook and decorate it however you wish.

If you are lucky enough to have an iPad you can create an online notebook using apps such as Paper by FiftyThree or Explain Everything.

TOP TIPS

Sketch ideas of what your den will look like.

Keep a list of materials you will need.

Include photos or pictures of dens that inspire you.

Keep a celebration gallery of all the dens you have built.

CARDBOARD
BOX
DENS

Grab yourself a huge cardboard box and with a little imagination you can turn it into almost anything! You can even use the same cardboard box to make lots of different dens.

YOU NEED

Large cardboard box (or more than one)

Masking tape

Thick felt pens

Fabric

Lights

Scissors

Clips or tape for fastening

TOP TIP

When you find a big cardboard box make sure you save it – perhaps you've had a new washing machine delivered to your house. If you ask politely at a local shop or supermarket they might save you one. If you need to store your box and not have it take up too much space, you can always flatten it and rebuild it when you are ready to use it.

What could you turn your box into? A spaceship, a shop, a castle, a house, a cave, a rocket, a garage, a hotel – it's up to you! You will find lots of different examples of cardboard box dens in this book to inspire you.

Get out some pens and pencils and start to design your den!

If it's a rocket, how might it look? You could draw on large numbers and add the name of your rocket. Perhaps you could stick on tinfoil plates as windows. Does it have a fuel cap, round windows or stars?

For some other ideas take a look at our rocket den (Project 5).

Does your den need a door or a window? How will you create these?

REMEMBER

Strong scissors work well on thick cardboard, but if you need to use a craft knife it is important to work with an adult.

TOP TIP

Take your cardboard box and just use two of the sides – this makes the base of a corner den which can go anywhere there is a corner. The hall, your bedroom … you decide!

We gave a group of den builders some cardboard boxes – just look at their creations!

Ella Mae wanted to decorate her cardboard box and add a 'roof' as well as some writing. The roof is made from material which is fastened with bulldog clips.

TOP TIP
Save old blankets or jumpers to make your den cosy.

What sort of material would you put on the floor of your den? Soft and floaty or snuggly and warm? What lighting will you use? A torch or some fairy lights?

Rosa wanted the box to be a fairy castle den so she could wear her dressing-up outfit in it.

Do you have your own dressing-up outfits? What sort of den could you make to wear them in? Will you be a pirate or a superhero? A dinosaur or a princess?

PROJECT 2
CASTLE DEN

YOU NEED

Large cardboard box

Scissors (or a grown-up with a craft knife)

Thick marker pen

Ball of string

Something to make a hole with

Take a large cardboard box and remove the lid section. Mark and cut out the turrets along the top of the box.

REMEMBER

If you are using a sharp cutting tool you must get a grown-up to help you.

Now cut out two slits for windows. Remember, you only need thin slits in your castle as these were used by archers to fire arrows through, which is why they were so narrow!

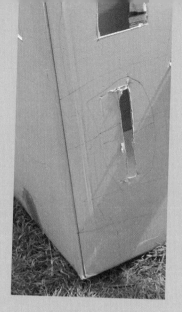

Next, cut out a door shape but make sure that you leave it fastened at the bottom – this will be your drawbridge. Make two holes in the wall of the box and two in your door. Thread your string through and tie a knot at each end.

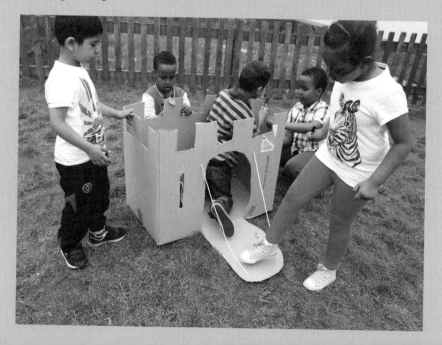

Finally, decorate the walls of your castle with your marker pen. What sort of stones do you think would be used to build a castle?

Will your castle have a moat? A flag? Extra towers? A warning sign for intruders?

And where will you position your castle so that it will be easy to defend from attackers?

Could you use the leftover cardboard to make costumes, crowns or swords that you can decorate?

How could you and your friends make an even bigger castle next time?

YOU NEED

Large cardboard box – opened up

Scissors (or a grown-up with a craft knife)

Torch or lights

Anything which you know has 'special powers' (non-spies won't know this!) – for example, an old keyboard or laptop, broken clock or watch, leads and cables, an old phone, special glasses

PROJECT 3
SPY DEN

Set up the opened out cardboard box in a corner so you have a frame with two or three sides. Make sure that you leave one side open as your entrance.

You now need to cover your den walls with lots of gadgets that non-spies won't understand. If you make holes in the cardboard you can 'plug' things straight into them to hold them in place. For shelves, you can push two pencils into the cardboard and then lay a piece of cardboard on top. Be careful you don't accidentally draw on the wall when you do this!

TOP TIP

Most grown-ups have a box of bits that they think might be useful one day. It could be in the garage or under the stairs. Ask them and you will be amazed at what they have stashed away – old computers and calculators make great spy den props!

An ordinary person might think that this is just the inside of a broken clock on top of a CD – but *we* know different, don't we? We know that it can transport you to the future (it's OK, we're not giving away any secrets!). What non-spies won't know is that it needs another machine to make it work (you must remember to keep that top-secret when you have made it!).

REMEMBER

Avoid using old gadgets with very small parts that could be accidentally swallowed. Never take apart electrical items unless you are with a grown-up.

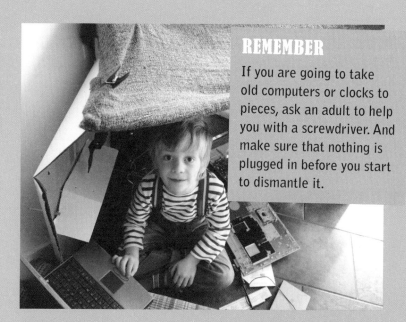

Once you have arranged your gadgets – on the floor, stuck into the cardboard or hanging from the top of the cardboard – you need some privacy! Cover your den with an old blanket – you don't want anyone guessing your secrets! Remember to use a torch and your special glasses when you are working.

WAIT! You should perhaps think about extra safety measures for your spy den – you don't want any non-spies or grown-ups wandering in by mistake, do you?

Set up a cunning obstacle just outside your den. It might begin as some string or elastic but *we* know it's really a laser system, which means that grown-ups won't be able to enter your den without your permission.

YOU NEED:
String or elastic
Torch or spotlight

REMEMBER

Always put your obstacle away when you are not using your den, and never put an obstruction at the top of stairs – you don't want anyone to fall over.

TOP TIP

Some 'spy equipment' can be bought. This plasma light costs around £15 but you could use it in lots of different dens – it would be great in a spaceship or a science den.

YOU NEED

Large cardboard box – opened up

Pencils to make holes with

Branches/twigs/leaves

Rustic material – sacks or an old brown or green jumper (ask first!)

PROJECT 4
NATURE DEN

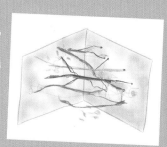

Open out your cardboard box to create
a two or three-sided frame (like you did
for the spy den in Project 3).
Make holes in the cardboard with a
pencil at different heights.

Head outside and collect
twigs and branches of
different sizes – some
with leaves on, some bare.

When you have decided where to place your den, begin to build the 'roof' by pushing the twigs through the holes you have made.

TOP TIP

It is a lot easier to make the holes with a pencil first and then push the twigs into them, rather than trying to make the holes with the twigs.

Once you have made a 'roof', cover it with more twigs and leaves. We have used some netting to provide a base for the leaves, or you could use material which fits in with your nature theme – such as hessian from an old sack or an unwanted brown woolly jumper or scarf.

Add plastic spiders and animals if you want to make it seem like a real nature den!

TOP TIP

See what natural materials you can find outside to decorate your nature den – a carpet made from leaves (if you brush PVA glue over your leaves they will stay shiny and not curl up as much) or a wall covered in pine cones or conkers hung up with string.

This is an ideal den to make for younger brothers or sisters. It's a good place to play with dinosaurs, spiders and farm animals.

PROJECT 5
ROCKET DEN

YOU NEED

Large cardboard box
Strong scissors
Pegs/sticky tape
Cellophane or clear plastic
OPTIONAL
Large sheet of white or black paper
Tinfoil
Glow-in-the-dark stars
Lights or torch

TOP TIP

DIY stores sell lining paper (which goes underneath wallpaper) very cheaply – a roll will go a long way and will cover more than one box.

Find a large cardboard box which is rectangular in shape – you need a tall box for it to look like a real rocket.

If you can find a white box that's great. If not, you can easily cover a brown box in white paper using sticky tape or pegs.

Once your box is covered in white paper, use a felt pen and mark the position of the main window.

TOP TIP

Fasten your white paper in place at the top of the box with pegs. Fold it under at the bottom and stick down with tape.

Next, cut out the circle to create your window.

Cover the hole with a circle of clear or tinted plastic and tape it to the inside of the box so that it is secure.

Now decorate your rocket with felt pens, coloured tape, tinfoil plates – whatever you have collected to make your rocket look amazing. You could use an umbrella for the pointed top and bright material and cellophane for the flames. You could even add lights and cardboard side fins.

Does your rocket have a name? If so, you could add that too.

If you make your rocket indoors you could draw a space scene on some cardboard and put it behind your rocket as a backdrop. Or you could use a sheet of black paper and make planets and stars from tinfoil, or buy a packet of glow-in-the-dark stars and stick these on or even tape lights on to the background.

What music would you play to set the scene as your rocket lifts off into space?

Where will your rocket take you?

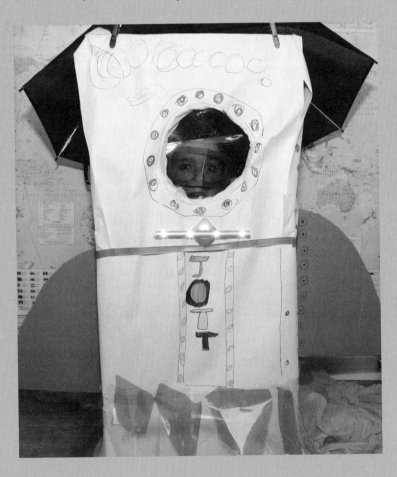

Remember, as a space traveller you will need some protective goggles. What other special equipment might you need in your rocket? How about covering an inflated balloon with papier mâché to make a space helmet?

REMEMBER

Young children should be very careful with small parts which could be accidentally swallowed.

You could make a control panel for your cockpit from bottle tops and broken clocks (see Project 3 on spy dens for some more ideas). Alternatively you could always draw your control panel.

Rocket equipment! What can you see in these pictures? Do you have similar items around your house that you could use in your rocket?

TOP TIP

Old CDs and DVDs are great for creating amazing colours – string them together and make a background mobile or stick them on to the side of your rocket.

Shine a torch and see what different effects you can get.

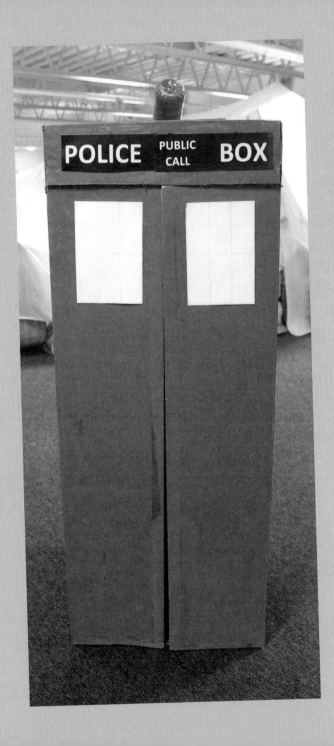

PROJECT 6
FAMOUS DEN

Now you have built a rocket and travelled through space, how else could you travel through time and space?

Do you recognise this famous den? Who did it belong to and why was it special?

Can you create your own version of Doctor Who's TARDIS? Look carefully – what has been used to make the light on the top of the box?

Can you think of any well-known castles, caves or hide-outs from stories or films? What other famous dens could you recreate?

PROJECT 7
SHOP DEN

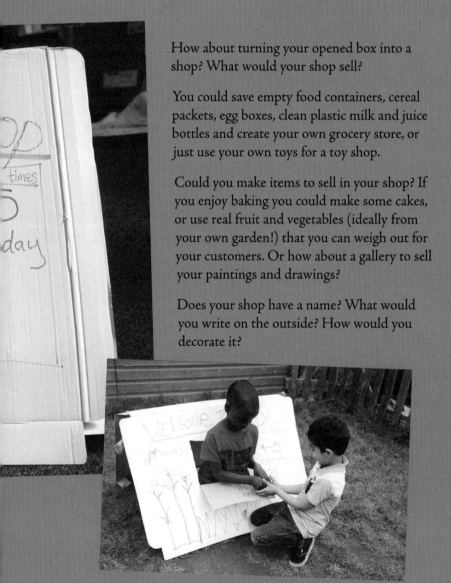

How about turning your opened box into a shop? What would your shop sell?

You could save empty food containers, cereal packets, egg boxes, clean plastic milk and juice bottles and create your own grocery store, or just use your own toys for a toy shop.

Could you make items to sell in your shop? If you enjoy baking you could make some cakes, or use real fruit and vegetables (ideally from your own garden!) that you can weigh out for your customers. Or how about a gallery to sell your paintings and drawings?

Does your shop have a name? What would you write on the outside? How would you decorate it?

TOP TIP

When you cut out your window, leave the bottom side attached to form a shelf for your calculator or till.

Could you be even more inventive with your shop? How about transforming your box into a vintage caravan selling teas and cakes? You could make (or buy) some bunting and string it from the box to a fence or some sticks. You could even have some tables and chairs or a blanket for your customers to sit down and enjoy their tea!

PROJECT 8
WEARABLE DEN

Can you find a cardboard box which is big enough for you to wear?

Tommy and Oliver are only little but with the help of grown-ups they became robots by using a cardboard box. If they sat down inside the box it became a den for them to peek through.

Young children love playing peek-a-boo, so could you build a den for a little brother or sister so their favourite toy can peek through the window at them?

With the addition of some shoulder straps (some string or ribbon) you could transform your box into a car, a ship or a train. You could also make yourself some accessories to go with your box – perhaps a pirate's hat or a train driver's peaked cap.

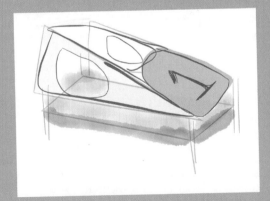

You could even be a building – like a beach hut, a circus tent or a farm building.

PROJECT 9
THINKING OUTSIDE THE BOX

TOP TIP

Look at the size and shape of your cardboard box – what does it suggest to you?

With a huge box like this one, you and a friend could design a side each!

TOP TIP

If you use chalk to draw your design, you can wipe it off later and create a completely new den!

Can you see what Ned is doing here? How is he creating his own shape on the side of his den? Could you do this and get a friend to draw around your outline?

Can you work out how Harry made his tank? What do you
think he used to create the camouflage? How does he get into it,
and how do you think he joined it together?

To make a tank like Harry's you will first need to find two
cardboard boxes of slightly different sizes. Cut a hole in the top
of the biggest box that is just large enough for you to fit through,
and then make a hole of the same size in the top and bottom of
the smaller box – make sure you leave the top circle attached so
that you can use it as a hatch.

Now attach the smaller box to the top of the larger one. We used double-sided tape, but how else could you fasten these boxes together? Now you will be able to climb into your tank.

Finally, find a small cardboard box and fasten a broom handle or tube to this to form the barrel of your tank. You can now camouflage your tank using paint or scraps of paper.

REMEMBER

Make sure that the end of your barrel doesn't have a sharp edge – you might want to add some foam or a plastic stopper like Harry has done.

What other types of den could you create by attaching boxes together? Could you make a tunnel? An underground cave? A lair for a monster?

YOU NEED

Large cardboard box – opened out

Black paper

Heavy duty scissors

Sticky tape

Chalk

Camera, tablet or smartphone

PROJECT 10
OPEN THE BOX

What can you do with your box when you want to take a den apart? If you open your box out flat, you have a whole new canvas to work with!

Cover one side of the box with black paper using sticky tape to hold it in place.

TOP TIP

It is easier to cover your box if you lay it flat on the floor.

Draw 'head size' ovals at different heights with chalk and cut these out with your strong scissors.

Then have some fun and draw cartoon bodies and figures around the ovals. We used chalk but you could use crayons or paint or stick on anything you wish.

Then all you need are willing friends and a camera! Sit back and enjoy everyone pulling faces.

You could do this for a special occasion such as a birthday party, Christmas or Halloween.

BABY DEN

Once you have finished with your 'gallery', you could turn it into a smaller den for a younger child or a baby. They love to have lights to look at, so fasten some small twinkly fairy lights to the black paper and then roll it up. Use a hula hoop to help it to stand up and add lots of tinfoil decoration. Put a cushion or a blanket on the floor for the baby to lie on.

REMEMBER

Always use lights that have been safety tested, and never leave a baby on their own in the den.

What could you design and create to hang from the ceiling of this den? Remember that babies like colour, sound and movement. Perhaps you could use lots of colourful pompoms or toys that play music. What ideas do you have?

TOP TIP

Save all the boxes and packaging that you use in a week. Add this to a selection of fastenings (see the resources section for some ideas) and some coloured pens, and you have all you need to build your miniature den.

PROJECT 11
MINIATURE DENS

Not all dens need to be human size – it's fun to make dens for your toys or favourite characters.

As miniature dens are smaller in scale, you can build them in your bedroom or the living room and they can stay there for a while. You could add extras as you collect more boxes, tags or colourful envelopes – anything that could be used to decorate your mini den. Save it all in a special den-making box!

Your den could be really simple, like Ned's robot den –
a cereal packet and a decorated label.

Or it could be a whole town of different buildings that your toys might use.

If you look closely at this miniature den, it was built in a box placed on its side. The den builder has used different types of paper, cut-out patterns from magazines, pipe cleaners, play-dough, pompoms and small boxes. It even has a chandelier and a duck pond – this is obviously a posh den!

Joe used tubes and boxes to make a tree for his monkey collection. The only things he needed to buy were the gaffer tape and the small spotlights.

TOP TIP

Old envelopes and tags make great leaves.

TOP TIP

Adding lights can make your den extra special.

Remember to decorate the outside of your miniature den too.

What sort of toys do you have?

Could you match the den to the toy?

PROJECT 12
MINIATURE TOWN

Once you have made dens for your toys or action figures, you could get together with your friends and combine all of your dens to make a miniature town!

Here is a miniature town in progress.

TOP TIP

Tiny sweet boxes make great market stalls or small shops.

REMEMBER

If you want to cut out small shapes or windows and need to use a craft knife, you MUST ask a grown-up for help.

You can add lights to really bring your miniature town to life – fairy lights or battery-powered candle lights are great for this.

TOP TIP

Use large sheets of cardboard as the base for your town – it will be easier to move it around.

TABLE DENS

All dens need a basic structure and the easiest way to create this is to use a table.

Move all of the chairs out of the way so you can get in and out easily, and remember to move anything on top of the table – breaking the family's best vase could get you into trouble!

You now have a 'roof' and four legs to decorate. Decide on your theme and have a look around the house to see what materials you can use.

The next two projects show you how to make a spooky table den and white table den, but look at the sketches here for some ideas for other table dens.

What materials would you use to make this underwater den? How do you think you could make the octopus and his tentacles? What fastenings would you use?

Look closely at this Viking longship den. What is different about how the table is used here? What could you use to make the shields, sail and decorations?

REMEMBER

Always ask before you use blankets or sheets. Some might be old ones that you can cut up but others might be special ones that you need to be very careful with.

TOP TIP

If you build a den at a special time of year – for example, Halloween or Christmas – you will be able to buy lots of materials and props very cheaply in pound shops. If you are very organised, buy them just after the event when they have been reduced – you can still build a spooky den in November!

Could you create a different den using an upside-down table? Sketch out some of your own ideas!

YOU NEED

Table

Large piece of material – we used a flimsy orange fabric (you can make pumpkins from this too!) OR table cloths from a pound shop

Black string and hula hoops to make webs

Lights

Black material for the floor

Masking tape/cable ties

Props – made or bought (e.g. hats, danger signs, masks, skeletons, pumpkins)

Finishing touch – stripy tights and boots

PROJECT 13
SPOOKY TABLE DEN

Have a look in shop windows and at retail displays during Halloween and start to note down some ideas for your spooky den in your sketchbook.

Now get creative and start dressing your table with the materials you have collected!

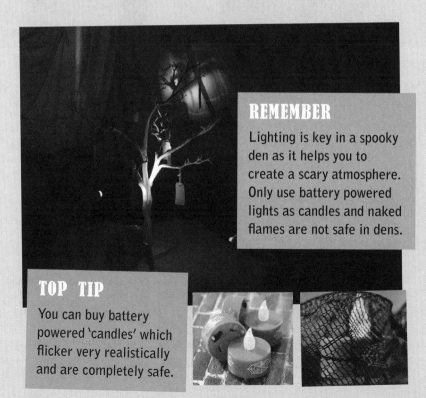

REMEMBER

Lighting is key in a spooky den as it helps you to create a scary atmosphere. Only use battery powered lights as candles and naked flames are not safe in dens.

TOP TIP

You can buy battery powered 'candles' which flicker very realistically and are completely safe.

Make the table legs part of your den! Stripy tights held up with masking tape and a pair of old boots or shoes (remember to ask) add to the spooky scene!

You can make spiderwebs using a hula hoop and black wool or string – you can then thread battery powered lights through this.

Make your own pumpkins by wrapping cushions in orange material and tying with string.

 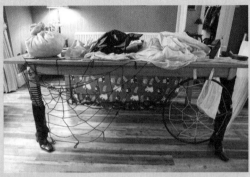

How will you customise your spooky den?

Could you construct your own skeleton? What sort of 'keep out' notices could you make? Where would you fasten them?

How dark do you want your den to be? Will you need to use a torch to enter your den?

Could you write your own ghost story to read to your friends in your den?

What music could you play to make your den even more spooky?

YOU NEED

Tinfoil, bubble wrap and thick sheets of clear plastic

Masking tape

White cushions and blankets

White fairy lights or rope lights

A silver insulating mat (you can buy survival blankets at most pound shops)

REMEMBER

Plastic sheets aren't safe for babies and small children – make sure they aren't left on their own with them.

REMEMBER

Use masking tape to fasten your materials as this won't leave a mark on the table when you peel it off.

PROJECT 14
WHITE TABLE DEN

Do you fancy making a table den but want one that is bright and white? Simply use the same table as you did for your spooky den, but swap your spooky materials for soft white materials like fluffy blankets or old jumpers.

Gather together your white and silvery materials and tape them to the table.

Turn off the room lights and use your rope lights only – then settle down for a chat with your friends or read a book!

What sort of music would suit your white den?

INDOOR DENS

Even if it's not raining outside, you can still make a great den indoors using the space and objects around you. Some of the dens in this section are quick and easy to make, while others are more complicated and draw on your creativity. What sort of den do you feel like making today?

PROJECT 15
LIVING ROOM DEN

None of these dens are fastened, and none of them took more than five minutes to make!

Put cushions or a blanket on the floor to make it comfortable, cover your den with a blanket or more cushions, and then snuggle down with a torch and read next to your granddad! How simple is that?

YOU NEED

Sofa or chairs

Cushions or blankets

Torch

Book

PROJECT 16
PADDLING POOL DEN

If you inflate your paddling pool, you have a ready-made base for your den. Obviously, if it's summer you can create your den outside, but if it's cold or rainy then use it inside – it will easily fit into your living room or bedroom.

Cover the base of the pool with a blanket or piece of material and fill it with whatever you choose. We used shredded paper, but you could use anything soft – from cushions to pompoms to foam balls!

You could hide your toys – or even yourself – in there!

REMEMBER

Be careful with your toys as the paddling pool will go down if you make a hole in it.

If this was a nest, who or what would live here?

Use your hula hoops as a frame – if you fasten two together they will 'sit' in your paddling pool and you can cover them with a blanket to make a roof.

YOU NEED

Your bedroom

Your prized possessions

Books, magazines and posters about your hobby

PROJECT 17
FASHION DEN

Think about turning a corner of your bedroom into a den for your hobbies. This one is all about fashion, jewellery and costumes.

This den uses a piece of red filmy material and props to create a chic den space. The shelves hold objects that fit with the fashion theme and posters and mirrors complete the effect.

How will you make your fashion den distinctive? Remember to light your den to suit your mood – perhaps using battery powered candles or fairy lights.

TOP TIP

You can easily hang material from a hula hoop which is firmly secured to a shelf with books or other heavy objects.

YOU NEED

Duvet (single is fine)

Two hula hoops

Bulldog clips (or cable ties)

Blanket

Lights

PROJECT 18
DUVET DENS

The duvet igloo den can be made in less than five minutes.

Well, what are you waiting for – go and grab a duvet!

Stand one of the hula hoops on its side – you might need someone to hold this for you. Wrap your duvet around this and secure it with bulldog clips. Repeat the process with the second hoop to make the other end of your duvet den.

REMEMBER

If you are using bulldog clips or cable ties, make sure you have a grown-up nearby to help you.

Put your blanket on the floor inside your den and light it how you wish. We used a colour changing LED light from a local DIY store. The blue setting fitted in with our igloo theme.

You can see here the two hula hoops – one at each end –
with the duvet pinned to them.

Wriggle in and read, listen to music or just have a chat!

As this is an igloo den it is white, but what else could you turn
your duvet into?

A volcano duvet den, of course!

First, pull out the stitching in your duvet. The stitches will be in lines, so if you snip one end carefully you should be able to pull out the thread quite easily.

Next, peg your duvet on to a washing line – this will make it easier to paint.

If you put your paint into plastic cartons (such as clean food containers), you can mix lots of different shades of red and orange to represent the lava.

Begin by painting an upside-down red and orange triangle at the top of the duvet for the lava, then paint shades of brown around it for the rock.

Flick your paint carefully to form specks of ash and lava.

Leave the duvet on the line to dry – if it looks like it might rain, cover it with a sheet of plastic or bin liners.

When it's dry, build your volcano den in the same way that you built the igloo den using hula hoops and clips.

Would you need any special clothing or eye protectors to go into a volcano? How could you make these? Could you alter a pair of sunglasses to become protective goggles? What material could you use to make a protective suit?

REMEMBER

Be careful when using plastic sheets and ask a grown-up to help.

What else could you turn your duvet into? A cave? A tunnel? The centre of the earth? The inside of a dragon? What ideas do you have?

PROJECT 19
SLEEPOVER DEN

You can turn your bed into a magical four-poster den by using four broom handles. Fasten these carefully to each corner of the bed and use them as a frame for your fabric decoration and lights.

Then invite your friends over for a movie and popcorn night!

TOP TIP

Lighting can change the mood of your den so think about using torches or fairy lights.

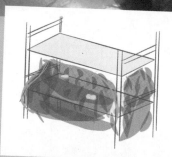

Alternatively, you could use some camouflage netting and create a secret hide-out in your bedroom!

PROJECT 20
DENS WITHOUT WALLS

A den can be created anywhere and made from anything – because it's yours, *you* make all of the decisions.

Does a den have to have solid walls? Not at all! These two dens show that you can create a special space simply using objects fastened to string and suspended from a hula hoop.

Do you love reading? It's really easy to create a reading den with objects strung from a hoop. This den uses pompoms and fairy lights.

Make several pompoms in different sizes and different colours.
Find a hula hoop and use this as the top of your den.

TOP TIP

Multi-coloured wool makes great pompoms. Most grown-ups will have learned how to make pompoms at school so ask them to teach you. Better still, get them to make some with you – then you will have lots!

While you are building your den, you might want to rest it on something so it's easier to tie on your pompoms. We used a clothes drier here.

TOP TIP

You can make pompoms using two cardboard discs with a hole in the middle, or you can buy special plastic pompom makers which speed up the process. Just search online for 'pompom makers' – they cost around £5 for a set.

Decide what you want on the floor of your den – you could use cushions, rugs, blankets or your favourite material.

Add lights to your hula hoop, and on the floor too if you like, then snuggle down with your favourite book.

TOP TIP

Have you tried reading by torchlight or with a special book light?

Instead of using pompoms to decorate your reading den,
you could create shapes from an old book.

REMEMBER

Only use old or damaged books
– and always ask first. Never
cut up or damage a book that
is in good condition.

Invite your friends into your reading den and ask them to share their favourite book suggestions.

Building a den outdoors – whether in a local park or wood or in your back garden – gives you the space and freedom to get really creative with natural materials and grand scale plans!

Outdoor dens are a great way to connect with nature – you will learn about the environment as well as the plants and animals that share the world with us.

OUTDOOR DENS

YOU NEED

Blanket or large piece of material

Five poles
(we used broom handles)

Ball of string

TOP TIP

You will need to work with a friend to put up the frame of your tepee.

PROJECT 21
TEPEE DENS

Use this sketch to help you set up the frame of your tepee den.

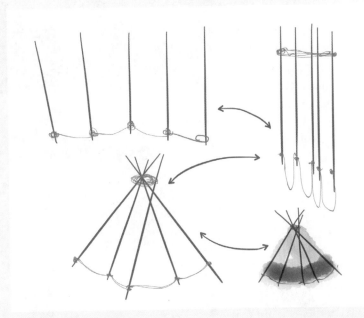

Lay the five poles on the floor an equal distance apart – you can use the length of your arm to measure if you haven't got a tape measure. Fasten these together with some wool or string by tying a knot at the bottom of each pole.

Stand the poles up and fasten securely at the top. You can then spread them apart at the bottom to create the base of your tepee. You should now have a solid framework which you can cover with a blanket and decorate however you wish.

TOP TIPS

We used a crochet blanket which meant it already had handy holes in it that we could use to secure it to the top of our tepee.

This den is easy to move as it is only fastened with string. Just fold it up and carry it to wherever you want to go!

Once you have the basic frame for your tepee you can create lots of different dens. What could you use to cover your tepee frame?

Here are some ideas from our sketchbook to get you started.

112

YOU NEED

A safe area outside

Twigs and branches

Different fastenings (see the resources section)

Waterproof covering for the floor

REMEMBER

'Take nothing but photographs, leave nothing but footprints.'

This is so important when you are building dens outside. You can use different fastenings to create your den, but you must never leave them behind as they could harm animals or plants and they can be bad for the environment.

PROJECT 22
OPEN-AIR DEN

Find a space that will suit your open-air den – it could be in your garden or your local park. Make sure you have enough space to build your den and that you won't be damaging any plants or animals.

TOP TIP

You could combine building your den with a nature hunt – don't forget to pack your magnifying glass!

REMEMBER

It is important to be safe – if you go to the local woods or park to build a den, you MUST take an adult with you.

Collect material that you can use to construct your den. You will
need to find a strong branch that you can use as a frame.

Secure your branch in place
– perhaps using a tree to
help create a solid structure.
We used tape here but you
could use string (remember
to take this home with you).
Then cover your frame with
twigs, leaves and dry grass.

Make sure you have some waterproof material (like an old tarpaulin or PVC-covered tablecloth) so that you can sit inside your den without getting damp.

Alternatively, you could build a den made completely from sticks. Think about how will you fasten it all together. How will you make sure it has a good solid structure?

You can also use material to create the sides of your open-air den. You can buy camouflage netting but it can be quite expensive.

TOP TIP

Large sheets, tablecloths or blankets can be used for covering your den. Try to save any old ones from home or visit a charity shop and see if you can buy some cheaply.

Outdoor dens give you lots of space to play with, so you can ask loads of friends to come and help you build!

TOP TIP

Open-air dens are great for picnics (but remember to take any litter home with you).

YOU NEED:

A whirligig (you might call this something else!)

Tent pegs or paper clips

Rolls of white paper or fabric

Umbrella

Plastic or a blanket to cover the floor (if necessary)

PROJECT 23
WHIRLIGIG DEN

Do you have one of those rotary clothes dryers in your garden? We always called them 'whirligigs'. These are great as you have a ready-made centre for an outdoor den which is easy to peg things on to – because that is what is was designed for.

This den is so quick and easy to make.

Peg your rolls of paper or fabric to the clothes dryer in long lengths that spread out to form a dome-type shape. Fasten these into the ground – you can use tent pegs if you have them or unfold some paperclips and use those instead. Place your umbrella right on the top and your plastic or blanket on the floor. That's it – your basic den!

To personalise your den you could draw on the paper, use colourful material instead of paper, make some vintage bunting or string up pompoms or lights.

TOP TIP

If you use a see-through umbrella – and wait for the sun to set – you will get magical natural lighting!

OR you can use dark material instead of white paper and add battery-powered tea lights or fairy lights.

REMEMBER

Umbrellas have sharp points so be careful!

PROJECT 24
UMBRELLA DEN

Not all dens need to be fastened down and in one place. Sometimes it's fun to made a den that you can move around while you are in it.

All you need for this den is a group of friends and some cheap plastic umbrellas in different colours.

How many different shapes
can you make together?

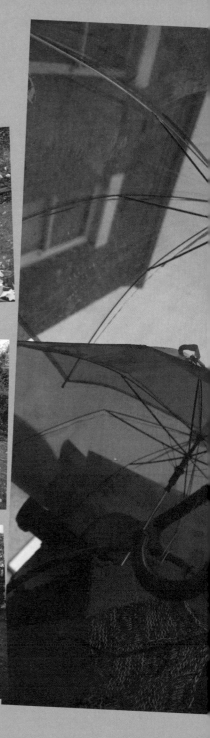

If it's a sunny day, see if you can make patterns with the light passing through the umbrella.

You can also decorate your umbrella with a permanent marker pen – or turn it into an individual den just for you!

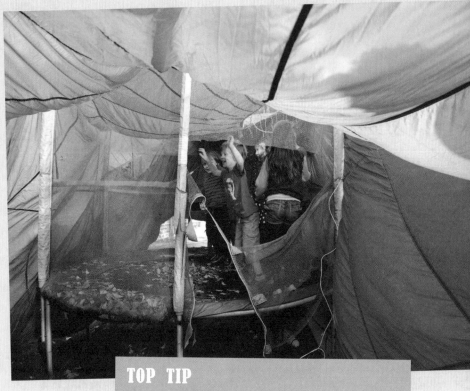

TOP TIP

Birthday present alert! Ask if you can have an old parachute for your birthday (have a look on eBay – they come in different colours and sizes). Print off some details and leave it lying around with hearts and smiley faces drawn on it!

PROJECT 25
TRAMPOLINE DEN

If you are lucky enough to have a trampoline in your garden then you have the frame for the quickest den ever! You simply need a large piece of material to throw over the top. We used an old parachute as these are huge.

YOU NEED:

A wall (or walls)

Washing line or string

Bricks

Hooks

Large pieces of cardboard

Bamboo or sticks

PROJECT 26
YARD DEN

You may have a yard at home rather than a garden or know someone who has. In a yard you can include outdoor buildings or walls as part of your den.

Create your structure by slotting pieces of cardboard together into a 'tepee' shape.

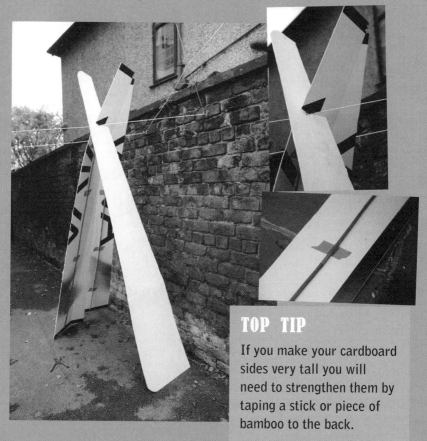

TOP TIP

If you make your cardboard sides very tall you will need to strengthen them by taping a stick or piece of bamboo to the back.

If you can, fasten your den to the wall with hooks and a washing line or string. You can wrap your washing line around a brick to hold your den in place.

TOP TIP

Walk around the outside of your house and identify new places that you could build a den.

You can then decorate the washing line with material, ribbons, pompoms, flags – anything which can be pegged to the line!

EXTREME DENS

PROJECT 27
EXTREME DENS

Now that you have worked your way through this book you will have developed your den building powers! Well done and welcome to the world of den builders. Give yourself a pat on the back and get your sketchbook out!

It's now time to be *really* creative and push yourself. Walt Disney said, 'If you dream it, you can do it' – and look what he created!

On these pages you will see some of the more complicated dens that we have made in the past. Look at these dens, take some ideas from them and then create your own masterpiece!

Can you tell what these dens have been made from? How do you think they have been constructed? What could you use to create variations of these dens?

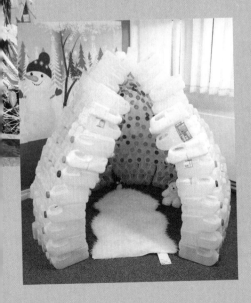

What will your extreme den look like?

If you could use all the creative skills you have learned throughout this book, what sort of den would you build? Where would you build it? What would be your theme? How would you decorate it? How would you light it?

Whatever your extreme den idea is –
make it, share it and enjoy it!

ACKNOWLEDGEMENTS

This book has evolved over time and as a result of many hours of creative play.

Thank you to family and friends for loaning us their children, their houses, their gardens and for giving up their time to help us. Many of you are featured throughout the book. We could not have done this without your support.

A special thanks to the staff and children at Pye Bank CE Primary School in Sheffield for trying out some of our ideas.

We would also like to thank the team at Crown House Publishing for having faith in our idea and for supporting us along the way.

13

21

25

31

35

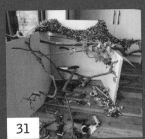

43

45

47

49

55

61

67

75

79

83

85

89

91

97

99

107

113

119

121

125

127

131